Snowlines

Rebecca Gethin

Rebecca Gethin

Maytree Press 2024

Published 2024 by Maytree Press

www.maytreepress.co.uk

Copyright © Rebecca Gethin 2024

The right of Rebecca Gethin to be identified as the author
of this work has been asserted by her in accordance with the
Copyright, Designs and Patents Act 1988

ISBN: 978-1-913508-39-5

A CIP catalogue record of this book is available from the
British Library.

Cover image: © David Coldwell

Maytree 048

Printed in the UK

To my beloved, Chris who accompanied me every step of the way, loved everything as much as me and believed in the wolves.

Contents:

In the foothills

darkness runs loose in the forest –
but at first can't break free from the brink
of trees. Finding escape from under leaves
it fills the valley like a flowing tide.

A nightjar flits back and forth.
Grass turns grey. Rocks shine.
A sprinkle of fireflies gives no colour.
A toad folds itself into shadow.

The other side of now never arrives
but keeps moving onwards
while constellations set sail
across clear waters of sky.

Footsteps

Once I thought words could describe this   Eavan Boland, *Translating the Word Home.*

Over the mountain top sun rises
slicing shadows into a geometry.
A man is walking uphill to the summit
as my grandfather did and all his brothers.

For a while it feels like I've returned
to a home I never knew I had
but the language isn't mine
and grammar sometimes stumbles.

If I could mix the colours of rock, scree
and snowmelt; of windblown scabious,
gentian and orchid, of sweet chestnut
and hornbeam in spring and autumn

would it help me translate the word *family*,
their photographs in the graveyard?
If I could draw lines of belonging
and see where they led

would it pigment the decades I've had no part in?
I once followed the paths from village to village
trying to make the tracks visible
as I mapped the old routes

so that if someone were walking home
in the dusk they could find their way.
In Italian, a path is *un sentiero*
and *sentire* is to feel: each one has its texture

under your sole, every bend passes a rock,
a tree or a drop. Sometimes a Madonna
bides in a shrine. The picture is glazed
by the river's rush, tinted with what I can't know.

Cima della Maledia

From the river valley
it was one step after another
as under our feet
a path to the col sprang to life –
a creature of habit that lifted us
at each twist and turn.

We followed where it led –
light and quick
across rumbles of scree
and over a lattice of trees
the snows pulled down
across the way.

Above, chamoix played
in the last of the snowfields.
You don't need to see
          avalanches
to believe in them.
So much to fear –
more than I'd thought.

Too far to turn back

1

Rain turned to hail beyond the lake.
Soon flakes the size of beech leaves
were falling. Above the tree line,
a whirligig blizzard. The way ahead

was a guess in ambiguous light
over boulders and scree, the hazard of snow
in eyes and throats – stumbling upwards
to reach a refuge. A broken sign pointed

to a cairn where a torn Italian flag thwacked
on a pole. Then a corner of corrugated roof
materialised out of thick greyness –
a crumbling place of safekeeping.

2

We opened the door and walked in to light,
a stove and a crowd of people. We said
Buona sera. A couple nodded.

Out there in the snow-cloud
there must be summits. Ground
of various kinds. A phone rang:

others were stuck higher up
in the blizzard. But tonight we'd made it,
had polenta to eat, a bunk with two blankets.

Later, I watched grey on white
drift towards nightfall. Mist fed off snow.
A stone clattered down the scree.

I spotted an orange glow: a man wearing red.
He waved, finished his cigarette and strode
away. Nightfall lightened as mist frayed

and snow-shine revealed crusted blue ice
in the abyss, the arc of a mountain
its tattered wings preying over us.

3

At first light I opened the door on immensity
    sunlight dazzled
far below *Lago delle Portette*
    stared like a Cyclops' eye
glacial sky struck
    the back of my retinas.

At breakfast things began to take shape
    two Germans said their lives were saved
by their rescuer who knew every cirque and hollow.
    All the others were Polish. We trod
in their bootfalls
    through the snowfields.

A herd of chamoix leaped
    across islands of ice on a lake.
A hairy caterpillar
    lay comatose on a drift.
The smallest melt-hole
    released a crocus.

What immensity is made of (1)

Baby water skaters cast shadows far
bigger than themselves: their pawlike marks
circle and circle, leaving no prints.
Damselflies chase one another,
flash their wings, their bodies a signal.
They cling tail to tail like stitches
their bodies arced into a loop of purl.
A water snake draws its pattern of markings
beneath a stone, its body listening.
Water trickles over a rock, etching a gully
deeper than a throat in a low gurgle
as of bees in a hive. Some butterflies
have blue fur. Others dance in the heat, land
on my hands, walk about to feel what I am,
curious to know what might give.

Schtum

i. *Monte Marguereis*

After the descent from the summit
from where mountain ranges lay like scrumpled sheets
thrown in a heap, I watched what I couldn't believe
defecating on the ridge above – its lupine
outline against the sky, the crouched back
and hang of tail, ear flick. At the refuge they said
No, not a wolf. They aren't in these parts.

ii. *Colle di Fenestrelle*

A sound like a gulp or a drip of meltwater
drew my eyes from the thawing path
beside the long fall of scree.
Footfall of chamoix perhaps?

Pebbled notes came again as a form flitted downhill,
barely visible with its stone-coloured pelt
but for that swift lope, the red hanging tongue.

I caught its reek. It fled from something
uphill of us, head turning once, eyes flicking back,
tail held low and still. Ragged and winter-starved.

I gagged the cry in my throat as I knew not to say
what I'd seen. In 1943 a thousand Jews
once crossed this border, heads turning back, eyes alert
and most witnesses stayed silent.

Superstition

Beside the *Torrente Gesso*
and not far from *Monte Gelas* (its name a curse)
we met two walkers under umbrellas.
They remarked on how we didn't seem
to mind rain. We asked if it might turn to thunder.
It'll be over soon if it comes at all.

We extended hands to one another
our arms about to cross in friendship
when she sprang back with a gasp
pulling back
her outstretched palm
before our fingers clasped a death.

La Valle Argentina

You know they are up there
where the stars stop:

mountain-shapes: blacker
forms in the darkness

where constellations pass
but can't shine through.

These are closer to you
than stars.

They have their own inner movements –
a smaller, more detailed

embroidery of mouse, adder,
beetle, innards, owls,

defecations.
Stars never bother

with things like that
but mountains have to.

The serpentine path from *Passo Garlenda*

Coming upon a shepherd boy sitting on a rock
at a lookout point as he kept watch
on his flock of tall Bregaschan sheep
was like walking into my grandfather's youth.

At first I wondered why this lad
wasn't in school but then thought
what more does someone who runs
straight down a mountain need to learn?

I took a photograph from below
when I thought he wouldn't notice
but when I enlarged the image later
I realised his eyes were glaring.

Fireflies

Out of the darkest point, from behind the house
and between the damson trees,
comes a prickle of light –

rising and dipping,
probing the fabric of air
for thin passageways to slip through.

Soon, one pinprick becomes a fleet
floating through night
leaving lightprints behind them
on the lume of darkness.

Monte Gerbonte's silhouette
with invisible flowers and grasses
rocks and landslides
is alive with sparks.

Their language is light.
A thunderstorm excites them
and rain can't extinguish them.
As if so many eyes opened then closed

in the dark. So brief: at the end –
a fading glim in a tail
a brown crackle
a beetle husk.

Lunambulism

The moon wildly gesticulates
at the river who insists
on keeping to its own place
in the channel despite shattered gleams
of light that singe the jelly-like surface.
But the water isn't able to carry them away
even when they are sloshed with spray
and the current fails repeatedly
to carry them downstream
for they aren't soluble, don't float or sink.
The noise is like a ceaseless scrunching
of paper, on which the moon scribbles words
in its mother tongue – white letters on a black
page – inviting everyone to their own wake.

What immensity is made of (2)

A hazel tree growing out of a crevice
casts a shadow of four leaves and a bud
on to the rock. A swallowtail no longer
has strength to lift its wings, flaps into
the bright water. Sifting the silt,
a speckled trout burrows through
the green weed grazed by tadpoles waiting
for their legs to grow. Listening to the trickle –
a benediction is about to happen,
is welling up – something
never stops coming to fruition.

Wading through landscape

Sunlight cuts a straight line
through evening shadows.

My knees feel a whiplash of blades.
Air thickens and sways, leaves shake:

in loose folds of the shade
a chiaroscuro reposes.

A patterned skin pulses, a spine
tightens, a script of venom flexes

inches from my foot. My heart leaps
the viper before I can name it

and now it's within me, behind my eyes
when I wake, spelling out what first detected me.

Tonewood

I wish we'd walked in the forests of spruce
high in the Alps where wood to make violins
grows tall and straight, a string section
of trees rooted in steepness.

If only we had – me loving the trees,
the shush and roar of wind,
you hearing the sway of notes under your fingers,
putting your ear to the trunks like the *forestier*

who listens for each one's ring from the heartwood;
the most resonant trees being felled in autumn
when the moon is furthest away
and sap sinks into ground.

We'd guess their ages and wonder
what histories the trees had lived through,
the fall of Napoleon, the rise of Fascism
and if effects of ice-bound winters,

droughts and storms were drawn
in their annular rings. We'd work out
the shapes of the rings inside us,
avoid calculating our survival rates.

Note: wood to make the best stringed instruments comes from the Alps which
provide the ideal conditions for spruce trees to grow

21

Disputed Borders

It's darker between scarps
where winter lives
than the darkness of sky.

Shadows move out
from under leafless spruce
like an owl's wing stretching.

Forms loom across the slopes
as if conflict had turned to air
looming across the land.

I Partigiani

Even a peasant girl could smile
and get through the checkpoint
and though not able to chat
she might bend her head for a light.

Even a *nonna* might carry a pistol
under her skirts as she poured a glass
or two of her rough wine
when they were searching.

Even a *bambino* might carry notes
from a village to a mountain pass
while singing *Ciao, Bella Ciao*
for a bite of chocolate.

Even reprisals didn't put them off
resisting occupation
of their own *orto* or *campo*
using their wiles like Trojan foals.

Hiding the Children

Speaking their names could spell
their end, burn the village to the ground,

execute those who homed them.
They can't utter their mother tongue

whisper *Mutti, Oma* or *Vater* –
not even to each other under the bed covers:

they must learn the village dialect
wear leather clogs, forget

the smocked dress and velvet short trousers.
They play near the soldiers

and translate what they pick up
about the whereabouts of guns,

the timing of raids, ambushes.
Called Marianna and Rodolfo now,

they must never ask why in the church
that man bleeds through nails on a cross.

What immensity is made of (3)

Rocks are mortal, crumbling
more slowly than flesh. A bee curls up
in a chink beside the water.
A thin current of water-snake
wriggles through the shallows
watching my shadow. Fish fry are wrinkles
of quickness, their underbellies
glint in the sun that revolves grey green
underwater. The bee's corpse floats
as the water skaters fight over it.
When I pick up three dead butterflies
my fingers are covered in ants.

La Chapelle Notre Dame des Fontaines

Shining out of the gloom
are the whites of Judas' eyes,
tongue protruding from his rictus;
Christ is being kissed
then nailed and crucified
while a tiny man is being dragged
from disembowelled entrails by a gryphon.

Faces in the crowds could be local people.
Look! A carpenter, a blacksmith,
a pious alderman - you'd recognise them all
though wearing medieval tunics,
pointed hats, hooded capes. Their lips are wet
with their Occitan babble.

Above the altar Mary rides a donkey
across an avenue that leads into a town,
the same avenue that still leads into La Brigue.
Soldiers are closing in on startled men
at work in the fields.

Eagle Owl

An unfamiliar call throbbed
in the gloaming: *hooo hoo* at regular intervals.

Bruno on his evening walk told me the dialect word
which I repeated till it was mine.

The name in my mouth conjured colours of feathers,
the pricked ears and far-seeing eyes.

He knew the words for the sneeze of *camosci*
when alarmed or the whistle of sentinel marmots

or the space at the back between house and rock.
He bred guinea pigs to eat, knew the smell

and worth of newly skinned wolf's pelt.
His door knocker was a trotter of a *cinghiale*.

He never said that partisans had used
the eagle owl's call as their signal.

If I asked about them, he shook his head
and said they were *briganti*.

Camosci is Italian for chamoix
Cinghiale is a wild boar

27

A corkscrew path

i. m. Carlo

We can't bring ourselves to open the last bottle in the back of the cupboard, made from the strawberry grapes that grew in radiant Alpine air, all rock and sky, the soil stony and wormless. The vines' short racemes of cream, scented flowerlets, pollinated by a hum of thousands, turned into fingernail-sized berries, as blue as nightfall, nothing but a squish of sweet-sharp juice among pips and skin. Pruned expertly each year by Carlo who picked all the palm-sized bunches at just the right time, as firm as clusters of muscle, gentling them into a barrow which he wheeled to his terrace. He pounded them to release a peony-dark liquid which he fermented into a wine. If you sat at his table, he never let you stop sampling his love potions: pink and crimson, maroon and amber, his kitchen and cellar being full of carboys, bottles and corks. He'd never let us leave until we were so laughed-out and wuzzy-worded we dizzied through the darkness, not sure if the zig-zag path was tilting more steeply or if we were steepness incarnate.

Eduardo

I first met him while he was having a slash
in the bushes below the church.

He shook my hand and I felt friendship
clasped by its knobbly geography.

He tended his bees in hollow tree trunks
and let them walk across his bare hands.

He gave us a big jar of honey, one of his last,
which we haven't yet opened. It's on a shelf.

He knew my father and his father. He hooshed
a breath and said it was risky back then.

He could tell me the names of those who built
the terraces on the steep slopes below us

where they grew potatoes and beans to survive.
He'd known the lads who tended goats and sheep

on high pastures, alone all day. On moonless nights
they hung on to a goat to guide them home.

During the war, his mother had buried her saucepans
which Mussolini demanded for weapons

while her brothers knew caves to hide from the enemy.
He said my bi-lingual father was too dangerous to know.

I muretti di luna

Mountain nights are dark as mouths of caves.
Then backlight brings shadows to life.
The Pleiades stream over the ridge
as though giving signal

to fireflies that ignite
from alleyway-darkness
catching the wave edge of stars
to search the high tide of night.

Stones gleam, chestnut leaves glint
as a greater light burns and burns
against the darkness: the moon's corona
inches over the ridge, sets sail across
the sky's clear waters.

Creatures that waken at night
and the steep slope underfoot
slipped into their dreams. Perhaps
there was shouting and singing.
Or was it silent?

Note: *i muretti di luna* (little walls of moonlight) are the terraces
built after dark and on land difficult to cultivate) on steep
mountainsides by peasants who grew their crops there after
the day's work for the local landowner.

Snowdrifts linger under *Passo della Mezzaluna* while cowslips flower

A hermit once lived in a cave and built a wall
across the mouth for shelter. Kept bees in a hive.
On the cliff face he chiselled a sailing ship,
angels and a face surrounded by thorns.

He wrote in Latin. Sometimes in blood
that didn't wash off. They left him food and oil
in a goatherd's hut. Knowing he was fearful
no one visited but they heard him singing.

In an empty village a water spout arcs
into a trough where someone once chiselled
a sun and a half-moon above a figure
with stick arms, quizzical eyes.

Around the blackened wick of a trunk
a corona of apples smoulders on the turf.
They wrinkle down – spent votives
for a deserted land.

Acknowledgements

Versions of these poems appeared in these magazines/anthologies:

In the foothills - Lovely, Dark and Deep anthology, Grey Hen Press
A Corkscrew Path - Spelt
Hiding Children - Prole
I Muretti di Luna - Lighting Out, Beautiful Dragons
Tonewood - The Poetry Village; Lovely, Dark and Deep anthology, Grey Hen Press

Heartfelt thanks to Bridget Thomasin for her wise advice and encouragement; to all my friends in Litmus and the Company of Poets who have read and commented on versions of these poems; to Chris, who loves the upper Valle Argentina and has accompanied me everywhere. Thank you to this beautiful area for being our sanctuary. And thanks to my grandfather who was born in Realdo, a village perched on a cliff high above the River Argentina. Thanks to David Coldwell at Maytree Press.